WILLING & ABLE

a true story of adoption

BY ELAINE CHISSICK

You don't have to share the same genes to be a family.

Elaine Chissick

I don't have a family tree, I have a Giant Redwood!.

Elaine Chissick

This book is dedicated to my family, all of you.

Preface

There's a lot of information out there concerning adoption, if you are willing to hunt it down and read through a whole lot of text to find the answers that you are looking for.

People tend to think that adopters are perfect and have everything. When I first mentioned adoption to my mother as an option to have a family, her first words to me were "They won't let you adopt, Elaine, you don't have any money."

But it's not just about money. It's about having the strength and determination to take on a child, and give them the best possible start in life, one that they probably would never have gotten if someone had not been there to adopt them.

So that's why I wrote this book, this is our story, this really happened, and I am passing it onto you so that you know what to expect and what to prepare for if you decided to adopt. It's not for everyone, but it was for me and Ray.

I hope you enjoy my story.

Elaine x

1

I met my husband in January 1994, in, of all places, a pub. He was rather an odd looking fellow, tired, drawn in and with no real sense of what life direction he was heading in - not really surprising considering the direction from which he had just come. At that time, he had living with him his 12-year-old daughter from his first marriage, and saw the children from his second marriage every other week, on a Sunday from 10 in the morning until six in the evening. That had stopped after a while at the hands of his ex-wife, then after a few years started up again for six months and then stopped again. After fighting it for so long, spending over £3,000.00 on solicitors and getting nowhere, he reluctantly gave up.

He had been divorced by his second wife and had recently set up home with his 12-year-old daughter from his first marriage (his first wife had divorced him and then passed away) and this was one of those occasions where she was at an auntie's house and he was out on the town.

Having recently lost my own house after leaving a somewhat "bad" relationship, I found myself living back at my parent's house, trying desperately to find my dignity and self-respect - something I had lost 6 months earlier.

We had a mutual friend who introduced us and after a drink and chat I agreed to go on one date with him. Three months later, I moved in with him and his 12 year old daughter. In July 1995 we got engaged and in June 1996 we were married.

During that first three months, the many nights we were together were spent talking about everyone and everything, putting the world to rights and challenging each other on how we would run things. It didn't matter that I was 20 and he was 35. We talked about getting married and having kids, something it turned out that we both wanted to do. We even talked about names and although we could never agree on a daughter's name, we both agreed that if we ever had a son he would be called James Joel Chissick. (Joel, after my step-father who had brought me up from the age of 2).

Not long after I moved in, his daughter accidentally mentioned to me that my husband-to-be had, in fact had a vasectomy! For a split second my world fell apart. His daughter saw the reaction on my face and immediately ran out of the house crying, to find her dad who was talking to one of the neighbours down the street, and did nothing but apologise all the way home. Which is what he went on to do for the next twenty-four hours. I had some thinking to do.

I had finally found my soul mate. The man I wanted to share the rest of my life with - was this one little thing really enough to break up such a good relationship?

No.

I thought, and we talked - there was

bound to be something we could do.

Six months before we got married we moved to a new house. It wasn't very big and I certainly started to feel cramped, but life went on. We made an appointment with my husband's doctor to talk about a vasectomy reversal. No good. After a certain amount of time, if the pipes are re-joined and sperm is produced, the male body thinks that the sperm is a foreign object, and attaches anti-bodies to it, rendering it helpless. The next problem was how had the vasectomy been done, had the pipes been snipped and tied back or had a chunk of pipe been removed before being tied back? Then there was the cost! Approximately twelve hundred pounds for the operation and no guarantees of a successful reversal - never mind a pregnancy.

"Not to worry" - I thought. Next we tried a local hospital for women. They told us of all the weird and wonderful things there were going to do to my body and my husband's body. The drugs we would be taking, the removal of eggs and sperm, putting the fertilized eggs back in me and even possible counselling should multiple embryos form, (in which case I would need to "possibly abort" some of them). Then there was the approximate two thousand pounds per treatment bills, and the fact that as a 'large lady' I was told to lose 2 stone before they would even consider taking me on - according to them, I was clinically obese! We returned home very downhearted, and as I relayed the conversation about having to lose weight to my mother, her first words were "well you will never be a mother then". Her cutting remarks registered at the back of my mind. They made me more determined to succeed in having my own family, but that was also to become the first in a long line of incidents that would eventually separate me from my mother and step-father in a way I could never have imagined at the time.

After a couple of years, and various talks to our local council about funding (none), counselling (none) and help (none) and adoption/fostering (they did not want to know) I found myself starting to realise that I was never going to have my own children. This thought was abruptly put on the back burner when in 1998 my husband had a heart attack. It happened on a Sunday afternoon whilst he was hoovering the car. I was ironing in my pyjamas at the time and as he staggered up the stairs with sweat dripping from him, I simply told him to stop messing around and leave me alone. When he fell into the bathroom and started moaning and throwing up I knew it was serious. So with the phone in one hand on a 999 call for an ambulance, I tried to get changed with the other. I also called a neighbour who pole-vaulted the adjoining fence, followed by his girlfriend, and was at my front door before I put down the phone. I was so glad as Iain stayed with my husband and Belle stayed with me. Believe it or not all I could think about was making sure I had a can of pop, a packet of crisps, mobile phone and house keys. I had no cash on me that day and did not know how long I was going to be away.

The ambulance finally came and whisked Ray and I off to the local accident and emergency where I was ushered into a relative's room and left alone.

After a time someone came in and told me that he was to be transferred to the intensive care unit and I could go with him. Once there they sat me in another room until they got him settled. Eventually, I was allowed to see him.

It took a few days for the results to show, but he had definitely had a heart attack and after seeing his consultant it was decided that he was to have a double heart bypass. Unfortunately we could be waiting up to a year for the operation and it was to be done in the City, as is could not be done in our local hospital.

So life went back to some normality and we waited. We didn't speak much about it and in December of that year I ended up on anti-depressants and sleeping tablets, unable to think of what life was going to be like if anything happened and I was left alone - and I was still under thirty! Then the feelings of not being a mother came bubbling back up to the surface. I couldn't bear to watch anything on the television that involved babies or pregnant women and whenever I saw someone in the street with a baby or a bump I crossed the road. I suddenly knew what must be going through the minds of the women who steal babies from maternity wards, as I really feel that I could have so easily done it too. For the first time in my life

I so desperately wanted to hear a voice say "mum" to me, and was so sure it was never going to happen.

My husband went on to have his operation, we got through that and came out of the other side better than ever - despite the fact that once on the operating table the consultant decided to do a triple bypass, my husband had to be taken back into theatre to be opened up for a second time as they could not stop his internal bleeding, and for a brief moment they could not tell me if he was alive or dead!

After three months he was back at work as if nothing had happened and once again the feeling in me of never being a mother crept back into the deepest filing cabinet in my brain and stayed there.

Then we moved house again. This time we bought a bigger house. Lounge, kitchen, big hallway, separate dining room, double drive, large back garden and three bedrooms and spent three years renovating. New kitchen, new bathroom, conservatory, eight new internal doors, knocked a fireplace down (it was very eighties), redecorated all but the spare room, built two decks in the garden, a gazebo and started work on a garden pond.

2

In the second week of April 2000 a work colleague's wife gave birth to a beautiful baby girl. I was really happy for them and, as the only female in the workplace, was left with the job of sorting out a gift. A trip to Mothercare followed and I even finished a cross stitch birth sampler for them and all was ay-ok. A week or so after Gill was born, the proud parents brought her in and I was utterly ashamed at myself for only standing in the doorway and looking on. She was offered to me to hold but I declined and made up some feeble excuse that I didn't want to drop her, then left and retreated back to my office where I spent the rest of the afternoon in tears. To Iain and Amy, if you ever read this book I am deeply sorry if my refusal to hold Gill at that time upset you in anyway, I am now sure you understand why I said no.

Following the upset and after talking to my husband, who tried his best to console me, we decided that something had to be done. There was a rotting hole inside me that could only be filled with children of our own. I took straight to the Yellow Pages and found an advertisement for a council based group from a county near to our own, who wanted to hear from people interested in fostering and adoption. I was straight on the phone to make an appointment.

Mavis came to see us within a week and our two-year journey began.

First of all we had to travel to a place about an hour and a half's drive away from where we live, to meet with a group of other like-minded people who were also looking to adopt. There were four of these 'first informal meetings' where we got to look at the ins and outs of adoption, what was expected of us and what course of action we were to take. The talks were held in the evenings and one full Saturday. There was always tea and biscuits, (and a buffet on the Saturday) and we all helped with the washing up. We started out as a group of six couples; one couple never made it to the first meeting and another couple didn't show after the first meeting, so a small group of four couples continued on.

The meetings were about many different subjects as well as what would happen after these had ended. Some of them were heart breaking. We talked a lot about the sort of children that are in care waiting for people like us to take them on offering loving secure homes. The sort of children that have been abused sexually, emotionally or physically, or had disabilities or had just been neglected by their birth families. The kind of care they received in foster homes, good or bad. The legalities of it all and also how we would cope being in the children's situations. I am a very strong-minded person but I don't mind telling you that a lot of my opinions were changed during that time. Being adopted by my step father myself, and not being told about it until I was 11, meant to me that I thought it was ok to keep it a secret. As far as I was concerned, I had no other dad than the one who adopted me and I thought this could work for every adopted child - I was wrong. I was only a baby when my mother and step father got together, but the children we are talking about are older and need to know where they came from, why they are where they are and that life will never go back to the way it was.

Whilst in these groups we did various exercises that got us thinking about the situations that we could be facing with our children. We tackled smacking (a definite no-no which I agree with anyway), we tackled showing emotions and family love to a sexually abused child, we tackled regression where a 6 year old child might go back to wanting to be treated like a 3 year old because of the time they had lost, and at each step of the way we were helped emotionally to deal with the strains that each subject put us under.

We met people who had children placed with them and the difficulties that they had gone through and we talked about 'our choices'. (Our choices being the kind of children we wanted).

At the end of these meetings we were given a form to sign to say that we wanted to progress onto the next level. All of us signed that form before we left the last meeting. Not one of us felt that we needed to take it home and think about it. All eight of us in that room wanted to press on.

What followed was a lot of form filling. Police checks, medical health checks, and CRB checks. (Everyone who works with children has to have one now). Because of my earlier mentioned weight problem and my husband's heart surgery we went through the medicals first as these were our main obstacles.

3

We then had an individual adoption worker assigned to us to do the home study course.

This is where your assigned Social Worker comes to visit you in your home on lots of occasions. As well as seeing you as a couple, your social worker will also see you individually, and will also meet with other members of your household, together with you, and on their own. The form that your social worker has to fill in, is commonly known as a 'Form 'F''. It's quite a hefty piece of work, and if you have a good social worker you will find that they will get many of the answers for this form from just talking with you during their visits. It's not unlike filling in a job application form, but more intense, the best way to get through this is by being open and honest. Ok, you are not going to agree with everything, it's your right to have your own opinions, and now is the time to talk them through and voice them.

Form F is divided into five main parts, questions included but not limited to include, in part one, your personal details, name, address, whether you want to foster or adopt, other people living in your house (children or adults). Details concerning your extended family, especially people who will have contact with the children placed with you, aunts, uncles, Grandma and Granddad, even close friends or neighbours can be included here. Part 1 will also include information about your education and work background, your medical information and details of people that you have asked to provide a personal reference for you. We had two couples who we asked to give us a personal reference, one of which was our very good friends Simon and Kayleigh, mainly because they had two young daughters who we used to borrow for days out to the seaside.

Part 2 deals with your cultural and religious background, especially important if you are in a multi-cultural relationship or come from a multi-cultural background yourself. Your social worker will also talk to you about how you and your partner's relationship work, as this forms part of the application too. Also looked at is your support network. Although our support network was small and mainly consisted of neighbours and a very small number of family members, our support network was a strong one. You will also be asked why you want to adopt children, don't worry about your answer, you may think is a silly one, trust me, it's not. One of the reasons we wanted to adopt, was because I wanted to be a mum, one reason we wanted to adopt a boy, is because Rays children from his previous marriages, are all girls, I wanted to continue the family name. This is also the time to talk about yourself, time to blow your own trumpet about your talents and your interests, and don't hold back. This part also deals with how you feel about asking to your children as they grow, about their background and where they come from. If you have concerns about this, talk to your social worker, that's what they are there for. This was a major stumbling point for me as I had grown up thinking of adoption as a taboo subject, and as my birth father as a "subject not to be discussed". It took me 36 years to find him, and I did it alone. I didn't want that for my children.

Part 3 deals with disability, of all shapes and sizes. And your experiences of disability, how to cope with it, and whether or not you accept it. Would you be comfortable and confident taking on a child with special educational needs? A blind child? A sexually abused child? A child with a life threatening illness? A child with behavioural problems? This is where you have to be really honest with yourself, you can't say yes to everything just to be a parent. Being a parent is about your happiness too, and wouldn't any child be better off with someone who is happy with who they have not just making do with any child for the sake of being a parent.

Part 4 summarises evidence that your social worker has seen that can go some way to showing how you can look after children, be it as part of your job, your family or your hobbies and interests. This is your way of showing that you understand the knowledge, experience and skills needed to become an adoptive parent. This part will also list any shortcomings that you and your social worker may have come across, and also any actions that you will be undertaking to rectify them.

Part 5 is a summary of the whole form, which includes a report from your social worker detailing your attitudes to birth parents. It also explains how well you worked alongside the adoption agency, your strengths and weaknesses and any areas of the home study course in which you experienced any difficulties.

Lastly, any points that you and your social worker disagree on are listed here, then you all sign the form.

The home study course is not just to fill in an application form; it's also to give you the chance to make sure that adoption is right for you. It gives you plenty of opportunities to ask any questions that you might need to ask. My advice?? If you think it, ask it!

Our social workers first visit was a nightmare, we were filled with upset, It seemed that all she wanted to talk about was the fact that I was fat, my husband had a bad back and there was the beginnings of a pond in our back garden, not to mention that she wanted us to sit round the table all office like and e-mail her our work before her next visit. She was very clinical, nothing like the warm friendly people we had met at the first set of meetings. She seemed to us, to dwell on all the negatives. This was not the way we were led to believe things would go and it left us with a bad taste in the mouth. Maybe it was just a huge clash of personalities, but it upset me and made us a little mad to say the least, and so I came to the decision that this was all wrong. The next morning I phoned the Adoption Agency and cancelled everything. My husband was quite annoyed, but understood, and said whatever I thought was right then he would stand by that. Later that day, my husband took a phone call from the Manager at the Adoption Agency and I got home from work that day to find that he had started it all up again! The Manager, Maggie, (a lovely woman) wanted to come and see us to try and work things out. It transpired that my husband wasn't just doing this to please me, as I had thought; he actually wanted us to have our own children just as much as I did, which came as a big relief as he had never actually told me that.

Maggie came, and was quite upset that we thought things were going pear shaped, and said that maybe this was just a storm in a tea-cup. As she said, our experiences in life and with Lucy (who was still living with us) were too good a thing to let go! She asked us to let her speak to the adoption worker and get her view on things and then see what she thought. My husband and I considered what she had said and decided this was only fair, and so agreed.

After a week or so Maggie came back to us with a proposal that she would like to set us up with a new adoption worker. Unfortunately this new worker was semi-retired and was doing this as a favour to Maggie, and as such she would not be able to see us until February. Although this put us back from the rest of the group by three months, we agreed. Melanie got in touch with us at the end of February and started her visits on March 12th, 2003.

The first half of our journey was over, but at that time it felt like it was just beginning!

At this time I had moved offices at work. Although I was still working for the same company, I was now working at the local head office in the City, this time with a group of girls including one named Terri, who was more my age. We got on really well and became good friends. Then she found out she was pregnant. At first I dreaded the prospect of working with my friend who just happened to be pregnant, but actually, this time it was different. We talked about all the feelings she was experiencing and for 5 months I watched her change from a stick thin girl into something that resembled the Mickey Mouse emblem on television. I told her so - she thought this very amusing. Terri 'let me in' on her pregnancy and was eager to show me her ever growing bump and whenever it moved at work she would call me over to feel it kick. My husband and I were even more shocked, but pleased when she and her husband asked us to be

Godparents. We didn't need any arm-twisting to accept the offer. While Terri talked about her bump, I talked about the various topics that we had been discussing with Melanie. Terri would listen intently as I rambled on about the latest subject that I had a different perspective on and then she would ramble about the latest colour schemes she was having for her baby's room, and if she was going to have a Winnie the Pooh theme or not.

We had a number of meetings with Melanie, mostly together, sometimes just me or my husband. We would chat about everything; she would drop questions in from time to time and would sit scribbling in her note pad while we rambled on and on. And believe me, we rambled. We talked about everything from the moment we were born, what type of childhood we had, what type or relationships we had been in, how we met, where we met, what food we liked what holidays we had been on, what football team we supported, what renovations we had done to the house, what we could offer a child, what we expected of our children, what pets we had had as youngsters, all kinds of abuse and the legal side of things. Most of the things which we had talked about in the earlier meetings we went through again with a very fine toothcomb and we talked about 'our choices'. The forms that had to be filled in by Melanie about us seemed endless and the final report came to seventeen pages. (When I read it now I almost believe that Melanie is psychic because I cannot remember telling her half the stuff that's in it).

We also had to give details to Melanie of two referees who would not mind talking to her and discussing what they thought of us and what kind of parents we would make. Ideally, these referees needed to have known us at least two years, as a couple, and have children of their own. So we chose our neighbours Sally and Jack, who have three children - although grown up - and Kayleigh and Simon who have two children - who from an early age have accompanied us on various trips and spent nights and weekends at our home.

Melanie visited our referees and my parents, and included these in her reports. Although we have a copy of the report about us, we have never seen the reports written from the information given by either of our referees or our doctor. Although after Melanie's visits, both our referees got in touch with us to give us a quick over-view of what had been said!

One last thing to mention on this subject was that Melanie also had to speak to my husband's ex-wife - that worried us. His divorce and subsequent battle to see his children had not exactly been a walk in the park. Melanie assured us that lots of people who wanted to adopt children were in similar situations to us, and what we needed to do was put our ultimate trust in her. I believe she made two phone calls the reply to one was "If you think I am helping them to adopt you can think again!" to which Melanie replied "I am neither asking for your help nor your approval, the decision we make will not rest only on your comments." She went on to ask the one question that she needed to ask and got the answer she needed to hear, then after another attempt to speak to her, the number was changed. As far as the ex-wife was concerned Melanie's job was over - she had evidence to show that she had sent letters that remained unanswered and transcripts of the phone calls so could go no further.

The question that she had to ask was "Had Ray ever abused his children?" His ex-wife's answer was "No."

4

As part of 'our choices' we discussed what we could and couldn't deal with in our children. We decided on a maximum age range of birth to 8th birthday (so 0 to 7). We said "no" to Aids, Leukaemia and any other disease that was life threatening but we said "yes" to diabetes or anything that could be treated with drug therapy. We said "yes" to a girl and boy, although we would consider two girls or two boys. We said "yes" to limited sexual abuse. We said "yes" to a child who wears glasses, "yes" to a child who was a little behind who, with help could catch up, and "yes" to a child whose parent had been shown to have learning difficulties or schizophrenia. But we said "no" to disabled children. These are hard choices to make but it is so important to be brutally honest with yourself and make the right choices. No matter what help is offered or changes made to the home, we just would not be able to care for a disabled, blind or deaf child. These are hard choices to make, but they have to be made. Our final choice was that we said we would take a maximum of three children. By this time Lucy had moved out and we had two spare bedrooms. And although Lucy will always have a special place in my heart, at 22, she needed her own space.

On the 14th June we had to travel quite a distance to attend a full day's course on Sexual Abuse Awareness. My husband and I were not looking forward to it at all. We all know it happens, we all have ideas in our heads about what goes on, but to sit in a room with 20 or so virtual strangers and talk about it was not nice. Discussing all the different words and phrases that are used to describe sexual abuse is not exactly an afternoon tea topic, but I must admit that it was not quite as bad as I originally thought. Although when we got into the car to go home I put my seat back, closed my eyes and tried to forget about the jack hammer that was going off in my head.

On one of Melanie's last visits of the home study course we talked about our family book, the book we would be making to introduce Ray and I to our children. As explained to the two of us, when children were found that could be placed with us, this book would be passed on to them, via their social worker, as an introduction so that they would have some idea of what we looked like before we met them. We started as soon as we could and I don't mind telling you I put my heart and soul into that book. By this time we had reached the end of the home study course and were waiting for the reports to be finalised so that they could be sent to panel, the group of people who were going to read all our reports and decide if we would be approved to adopt children. Maggie came to see us once again on 29th August 2003 to do her final report, basically to go over what Melanie had done and to see if we were happy with the way things were going. We were more than happy and now wanted to press on. We had decided that we would like to attend the panel meeting and Maggie told us that we would be hearing from them in due course as to the date of the meeting. All we had to do now was wait.

I purchased a black ring bound book with quite a lot of thick black paper pages from my local craft shop along with a basket full of different stickers and a couple of proper gold and silver pens (you know, the ones that are about seven pounds each and you have to shake them to get them going, none of this gel ink rubbish). When I got home I sifted through piles of photos and pulled out four ONLY FOUR! "Well," I thought "That's a really good start." I decided a field trip was in order, loaded my camera and set off with my husband looking at me as if I was crazy. I took pictures of everything, our family, every room in our home, the local park, the town park, the referees who were going to be aunties and uncles, our pet cat, who looked at me equally puzzled, the garden, the front of the house. I even e-mailed my uncle in New Zealand and asked him to send some pictures over. Then I took to the Internet and printed out a couple of small line drawn maps of the world and New Zealand so I could show how far away my uncle lives. I even got my mother, my neighbour and Terri to write a letter to these yet unknown children welcoming them to the family. After a week or so I sat down at our bedroom desk with all this stuff cluttered round me and began.

As I wanted this to continue after our children arrived I only filled the first fifteen or so pages, then made a note to the children that the rest of the book was empty because I wanted us to fill it as a family after they had arrived. Everybody who has seen our family book thinks it is great.

We received notice of our panel date - 18th September 2003.

I finished my family book the night before; I was determined to take it with me.

Melanie came to see us on the 17th to set things out for the next day. Maggie was also going to be there on our behalf and there would be 12 people on the panel. We talked about who they were, ranging from professional, legal and medical people to people who worked in childcare, people who were adopters and people who had been adopted. That's when the butterflies started! These complete strangers were going to make a decision that could change our lives or break our hearts.

5

On the day of the panel hearing, the plan was that we were to meet Melanie at a local Little Chef for a coffee, chat and perhaps breakfast. From there we would all go in her car to save us getting lost. After panel we would go back to the little chef and then home.

Due to a misunderstanding, we ended up at the wrong Little Chef. After a frantic phone call we were back on course and arrived at the right place to meet Melanie with just enough time to jump out of our car and into hers. We reached our destination in good time and had a quick coffee (and for me a sausage sandwich as I missed breakfast at home) and waited for Maggie. On her arrival we were ushered into a waiting room. After a while the panel chairperson came in and asked us a few questions, then, we followed him into a room where the rest of the panel were waiting, and were told where to sit. We were all sat at an oblong table. Some of the faces looking back at us seemed happy, and some seemed downright miserable, then the chairperson spoke. He introduced himself and passed to the person next to him who did the same, it carried on round in my direction. When it came to us, my husband and I simply nodded and looked straight to the next new face in the room, waiting for their introduction. After a brief silent moment, the chairperson said "ok, so you are... Ray and Elaine......." We suddenly realised that we were strangers to them and should be introducing ourselves - everyone thought this was quite funny and a stifled laughter went round the table. The rest of the panel introduced themselves and we got down to business. We were asked a couple of questions, and Melanie helped us out when necessary, as she knows what we are like for rambling. (We had asked her to shut us up if necessary, but she didn't need to).

After what seemed like hours, probably only fifteen minutes at the most, we were asked to leave and go back into the waiting room. Melanie and Maggie had to stay behind for further discussions. My husband and I sat in that room and read every poster at least four times, and hardly spoke. The wait was awful. Had we answered their questions correctly? Did they think we were not good enough? Had they understood our explanations? Could we not go back in and re-hash our answers?

Again, time stopped and after what seemed an age, in fact only a matter of ten minutes or so, the door to the room opened a crack and the smiling faces of Maggie and Melanie appeared. I can't remember who said it but I know someone said, "You've done it, you are approved!". "Of course this is pending confirmation by the agency decision maker."

As they entered the room all I could think of was hugging everyone in sight. I hugged both Melanie and Maggie; I could not believe what I was hearing. They then told us that the decision was unanimous. Every person on that panel had agreed to approve us to adopt children; the only thing they could not agree on was age and number. They had finally agreed on children aged nought to 8th birthday, girls and/or boys, two, with a possibility of a third at a later date. I could not believe my ears; finally I was going to be a mother!

We became Godparents to Terri's baby boy Richard on 19th October 2003, while we waited to hear news of children for us. Months passed with one visit from Melanie on 15th January, when Melanie mentioned something about two sets of two boys; no ages or names were said. I think she saw that I was holding out for a boy and a girl, and the boys were never spoken of again. By this time my husband was convinced that we would get a young child and that we would be changing nappies, I was not so sure, I was expecting something along the lines of a 5 and 7 year old, not getting my hopes up just in case because I too wanted a young child. But we knew we were getting children and we knew their rough ages so on 12th January we visited the local school which I had attended, and secured a couple of places in readiness.

6

On Sunday 15th February 2004 I was sat watching a re-run of the Vicar of Dibley on Sky television. It was about ten in the evening; I had my cross stitch hoop in one hand and had put this on my knee to pay attention to the screen. It was a particularly funny episode where Hugo and Alice get married, you know, the one with the flashing tiara. Anyway, I was laughing so much for the first time in months that even my husband, who was in the bath at the time, could hear me. The phone rang, I turned down the volume on the television, picked up the phone and said "Hello?" I knew the voice on the other end but it took a few minutes to register.

"Oh hi Melanie, is everything ok?"

"Yes," came the answer, "I have something you may be interested in."

I listened intently as she told me of a girl and a boy who were looking for a new mum and dad. They were brother and sister, and their social worker had read our papers and wanted to see if we would like to read the reports on them. I listened intently at the little information that Melanie had at that moment in time. "Any names and ages?" I asked. For months my husband and I had joked about ending up with children called Mabel and Humphrey, or Cecil and Cedric.

"The little girls' name is Julie and she is five," Melanie said.

"Thank God," I thought; a wonderful name. Then I prepared myself for a seven year old and Melanie said "And the little boy is 20 months, and his name is James."

How I stayed on that chair I will never know. As Melanie had been speaking, I had been writing this bit of information on the back of my cross stitch pattern and at that moment my husband's head popped round the door. He saw I was still on the phone and was mouthing at me "Who is it, who is it?" I smiled, waved the paper frantically at him to tell him to keep quiet and carried on talking to Melanie. "Yes, yes, send them through; my husband is away though for a week so, yes, you could come on 25th February, yes ok, bye."

I put the phone down and relayed the whole call to my husband. He suddenly became this infantile idiot jumping round the room like a kid with his pants on fire.

On the 18th February my husband left on a business trip through Europe with a number of work colleagues, and when I arrived home from work the next evening, the children's reports were waiting for me. As soon as I had fed the cat I put the kettle on and sat down to some intensive reading. First Julie's, and then James'. I could not believe what I was reading, and I don't mind telling you I had to get the tissues out before I got halfway through. Another cup of tea followed, but this time I took the report into the kitchen, reading as I went - narrowly missing the kitchen doorframe with my head, so heavily absorbed was I in these papers, papers about my children. I suddenly had this overwhelming desire to telephone Melanie and tell her to go ahead, right then and there.

I needed a break. I put the papers on the settee and went upstairs to change into my pyjamas. After brushing my teeth and taking my earrings out I went back downstairs to find that Lucy and her partner had come in. They were considering going down to the local pub but didn't want to leave me on my own. I told them to get themselves off, after all I am a grown woman who has a thing about always having the doors locked, besides which, I had to finish reading these reports and I needed peace and quiet. After much deliberation (and pushing on my part) I persuaded Lucy and her partner to get changed and enjoy their night out. They did and once again I was left to my papers and my heartstrings.

It was about eleven that evening when the phone rang, I picked up the cordless and sat back down; it was my husband on the other end. He asked if Melanie had dropped of the reports as promised and I proceeded to give him a quick overview of the children's situations, before he could say anything I closed my eyes and said "I want these children." his reply contained something about letting him get home to read the reports for himself but I forged ahead, "I want these children, I just know they are right for us." In the end I agreed not to do anything until he had come home and read the reports for himself. I guessed it was only fair as these would be his children too.

My husband came home on 21st February, late evening. I had spent the few days in-between going over those reports memorising my children's dates of births and wondering what sorts of things they liked to do, Julie had been described as an obese couch potato and James had been described as a happy child who at 11 weeks old had gone into drug withdrawal and spent the next three months doing 'cold turkey', although the medical examiners had found no immediate damage, they could not say if there were to be any long term effects, whoever adopted these children would have to wait and see.

My husband read the reports the moment he entered the house, and I put on the kettle and began unpacking his things and sorting out the dirty washing, it was only later that I got to hear about his snowmobile accident - apparently a tree jumped out in front of him! We went over the reports again and talked about questions that we wanted to ask when we next saw Melanie.

Melanie arrived on the 25th February and one of her first questions was "What do you think?"

As soon as I had made a cup of tea, my husband and I sat down and said "Yes, let's go ahead."

She had gotten a little more information from the children's social worker and told us what she knew, we talked about the foster home that they were currently living in and what we needed to do now.

Melanie explained that the children's social worker had read our reports and wanted to come and see us. We had no objections to this and a couple of days later Melanie phoned me with a date. Friday 5th March.

Melanie came to the house with Anna - the children's social worker. My husband let them both in the front door whilst I was putting the kettle on in the kitchen which can be seen from the hall, I was due to go to work that afternoon and was therefore wearing my uniform, a long, navy blue straight skirt and a blue and white shirt - tucked in. In a later conversation about weight, Anna told me that when she first saw me in the kitchen she wondered who I was, as from reading my report she was expecting someone twice my size!

We went into the living room, sat down and began. Anna had been working closely with Julie, and had brought along some of her artwork to show us. She explained about the work she was doing, why she was doing it and to what end she was hoping to get. We talked about our hopeful plans for the future and the unbelievable coincidence of having a son named James. We talked about changing their middle names and surnames, what colours Julie liked and what would happen now. If Anna agreed that we were a good match, then she would have to write a report and go back to panel with Melanie and get their approval for a placement to take place. We were not allowed to attend that panel. At the end of the session Anna suddenly said, "I have some photos if you would like to look?"

We were a little surprised that things were going this quickly after all; we had been at this for nearly 17 months. Unbeknown to us, during the previous six weeks or so, there had been a lot going on between Melanie and Anna in preparation for their visit to us. Anna had the report about us, and Melanie had the reports about the children and both had been going through them with fine-tooth combs. When we did meet Anna for the first time, there was still nothing set in stone with regard to the children coming to us, we were offered photos knowing that there could still be various obstacles in our way, but chose to take the chance, and the pictures.

We suddenly found ourselves riveted to our seats looking at Melanie as if for approval, she took hold of Anna's hand while Anna still had it in her bag, "Are you sure this is going ahead?" She asked.

"Oh yes," was Anna's answer "I was 95% sure after reading the reports, I just needed this visit to confirm my thoughts."

"Oh, right." Melanie let go of Anna's hand and she slipped the pictures into mine. I could not believe that I was looking at photos of my children.

Imagine being pregnant and seeing your baby's scan picture for the first time. I can only think that that is how it felt, except I was looking at photos of a five year old and a 22 month old in glorious Technicolor! Julie with her long brown hair with blond tips in pigtails and James with his dirty blond curly locks, both with cheeky smiles looking as I can only describe as like two 'normal' kids. I was already thinking ahead to not putting her hair in pigtails anymore and cutting James' hair really short!

My husband and I sifted through the pictures as Anna said we could choose some to keep. We chose individual photos of each of the children and one where they were together. These photos are still stuck on my kitchen cupboard door and are a constant reminder of how much they have changed.

Both Melanie and Anna were convinced that we should have no problem at panel but we decided to wait until the last minute before we started getting their rooms ready.

The beginning of March came round - my step father's birthday, I really wanted to include Julie and James' names on the card but didn't. The last thing I wanted to do was jinx the whole thing. By now we had a date for Matching Panel of 15th April 2004 and once again we were waiting.

8

On 19th March Lucy moved out. She had found a place just up the road from us. She moved in with her partner and we helped as much as we could. She took with her our spare double bed and the two chairs from our three-piece suite. We had ordered a new leather two and three seater at the beginning of the year and had offered her our old one - however, we were still waiting delivery.

We helped Lucy in lots of ways over the next week or so, taking her to different places to shop for curtains etc. and spent hours taking them up and re-stitching them, we bought crockery and a toaster and reminded her that she needed towels and cutlery, we wanted to do as much as we could to ensure that she wasn't being pushed out by the arrival of her two new siblings.

Around this time - I cannot remember the exact date - Anna set up a meeting between the foster carers and us. We met at a café in the town joined to the offices of the Adoption Agency and were pleasantly surprised. I think we all have our ideas of what foster carers are like but sat in front of us telling us about our children were two absolutely wonderful people. They told us about their typical day, what the children are like, how they act and the things they say, it also dispelled some of the myths that we had heard about foster carers at the beginning of our long journey. I still cannot understand people who foster, it's such a hard and demanding job, you could be looking after children for years or days, they could even go back to their birth parents, I know I could not do it. Medals should be given to those that can do it and do it well.

Then we started redecorating our two now empty bedrooms in readiness. Anna had told us that Julie liked the colour pink, and as James was a boy we opted for blue for his room. In ten days, we stripped, filled holes, primed and glossed wood, re-papered, hung new curtains and had new carpets fitted in the two rooms. Julie's room was very pink. We chose a lovely pink paper embossed with pink and silver filigree hearts, a red carpet and cream curtains (cream to tone down the pink!) Everyone who walked in that room remarked how pink it was, by the end of the week I swore I would throw the brush at the next person who said, "Do you know it's pink?"

For James' room we had a light denim blue carpet fitted. On the bottom half of the walls we used a textured denim blue paper and on the top half we used cream paper with blue squares and silver squiggles, we have ceiling fans in all the rooms except James' so my mother bought him a Bob the Builder up-lighter.

At that time, we had still not been to Matching Panel so my husband flatly refused to let my buy anything personalised. (I wanted to buy name plates for their doors). But we did start to look at equipment. After trudging round numerous so-called discount baby stores, we ended up in Mothercare. It turned out to be the cheapest, and that afternoon we walked out with a car seat that turns into a booster cushion, a pram and a high chair, later we went back for cot sheets and a cot quilt, on the next trip it was melamine Thomas the Tank Engine plates dishes and Fimbles cutlery. I could not believe that I was in Mothercare purchasing items for my children. We kept the sales assistant busy for a good thirty minutes going through the different car seats and looking at the different prams and how they folded. She was an extremely nice woman; we walked out with our goods, a Mothercare store card and 20% off our £200.00 bill.

9

On 15th April, the day before Matching Panel, I phoned Melanie to 'wish us luck' and found that she had been taken ill. Maggie, the Manager was going to be attending Panel with Anna and would phone me as soon as it was over. I started to panic.

I had completed all the adoption leave arrangements at work and was due to finish work on 16th April, the day after panel, I was suddenly extremely worried that things would go pear shaped and I would have to stay at work and re-arrange everything at the last minute. Maggie had got my work number to let me know and so every time the phone rang, my heart skipped a beat.

When I did finally get a call from Maggie it was not quite what I wanted to hear! The panel had agreed the match in principal but they had a few questions - one was about finance. We had not filled in the appropriate forms to apply for an adoption allowance. As this is means tested we knew we would not be eligible so didn't bother, the panel wanted us to fill it in anyway. They also wanted to clear up a question regarding contact between the children and any members of their birth family. This was really nothing to do with us personally but the panel needed clarification - although at that time, many of the family members that were known about were quite elusive! The decision now rested with an agency decision maker who has the final say. As Maggie explained to me, it could go one of two ways. Either, the decision maker would say yes go ahead with the introductions and placement, or no, wait four weeks, get the new information and go back to panel.

We had an agonising 24 hours wait.

On Friday 16th April 2004 my manager

Judith did a special buffet lunch to wish me luck and gifts were presented to me. They had put together and got me an absolutely gorgeous 3D picture in a gold frame of three calla lilies made from clay, a basket of flowers, a Dicentra for the garden and a wonderful card. Knowing my passion for chocolates my boss also gave me a box of Terry's All Gold. All this and I still was not sure if we were going ahead with the introductions.

Late that afternoon, I got the call I was waiting for. The agency decision maker had decided in our favour. The other matters still had to go back to panel but they had no major bearing on the decision to let Julie and James be placed with us.

From here, the next two weeks were hectic. I have recorded them in diary form so that you get some idea of what happened, but I would just like to mention that in-between visits and shopping my husband also laid a deck on the back garden and fenced off, using a deck handrail, the crater that was to become our garden fish pond.

Tue 20ᵗʰ April

Arrive at Adoption Offices for a meeting with Sarah (who has now taken over from

Melanie on our behalf - another lovely woman) Anna, Marty (Anna's boss) and the foster carers to discuss the actions of the next two weeks. In a couple of hours we will meet our children for the very first time. Various forms are filled in and a two-week plan is formulated with who is driving where. The foster carers then leave and we talk with Anna and grab some lunch. At half past one Anna takes us in her car to the foster home and we meet our children. We are very nervous. Julie is very quiet but begins to talk after Anna gets out our family book that she had been showing Julie the day before. James is, just James. Typical carefree toddler, toddling around and showing us all his toys. It is a quick visit and we leave after half an hour. *Today we travelled 64 miles.*

Wed 21st April

We leave home at 2.45pm. We see both the children and start to interact. I have a quick chat with foster mum and realise that I need to start stocking up on nappies, baby wipes, nappy bags etc, etc. I read my first story to Julie on this day, Cinderella. The foster mum is really good and tends to leave us in the room to get on with it. Today I changed my first nappy!!! Arrive home at 7.15pm. *Today we travelled 78 miles.*

Thu 22nd April

We leave home at 12.15pm and arrive at the adoption offices for a meeting called 'Life Appreciation Day'. This is with Anna, Sarah, Marty, the foster carers and us. We talk all about the children's birth family. The who's, why's and wherefores of their lives up to now. We arrive to see the children at 6pm and get home for 8pm. *Today we travelled 71 miles*

Fri 23rd April

We leave home at 12.45pm and arrive at the foster home at 2.00pm to spend some one-to-one time with James, who loves nothing more than bringing you a book or a toy car to look at. We go to Julie's school with the foster mum and meet Julie's teacher who is glad to meet us, then we walk back to the foster home, with me pushing James in his pram. We leave at 6.45pm and arrive back home at 8pm. *Today we travelled 109 miles.*

Sat 24th April

We leave home at 12.15 and arrive at the foster home at 1.30pm. We have fitted our car seat and decide to take the children out for something to eat at McDonalds. We go back to the foster home and play with the children and their toys and start talking to the foster carers about moving some of the children's belongings. We fill the boot with what we can, and arrange to take our sports bags with us sometime next week. We take part in the children's bedtime routine and put them to bed at 7.00pm. We leave the foster carers and arrive home at 8.15pm. After unloading the car (and having a quick play with the toys) we have a microwave curry and go straight to bed. *Today we travelled 174 miles.*

Sun 25th April

Leave home at 10.15am and arrive at foster home at 11.30am. We visit a local Park and take the children out for lunch. We get back to the foster home and spend time talking and playing with the children. We go through their bath time routine, get them ready for bed and say goodnight at 7.00pm. We leave and arrive home at 8.15pm. *Today we travelled 109 miles.*

Mon 26th April

Left home at 12.45pm and arrived at the foster home at 2.00pm. We spend some one-to-one time with James and then took him to school to collect Julie. This time we went on our own. I can't quite decide if the look on Julie's face is one of happiness or sadness when she realises that we have come to pick her up on our own. I put it down to a mix of the two, as I know she is upset at the prospect of leaving her friends. We arrive back at the foster home and sit with the children while they have their tea. It's a wet rainy day so we stay in the house and leave after we have taken them to bed. We arrive home at 8.15pm. *Today we travelled 80 miles.*

Tues 27th April

This is the day when our children see their new home for the first time. I am up with the larks hoovering, dusting and making the place generally tidy. The only thing out of place is the garden pond, which, although safe, is still a hole at the moment. Anna arrives at 9.30am with Julie, James and the foster carers. We have been continually bringing home various bits and pieces from the foster home and the children are happy to see some of their toys waiting for them. They look round the house at their bedrooms. Julie is excited about having her own room as she is sharing a room with James at the foster home. She is also quite surprised that we know her favourite colour is pink. She falls in love with the feathered wings, halo and pink feather boa that is hanging on the back of her bedroom door and spends the entire visit walking round dressed up as an angel. They leave at 12.00noon. By this time we are walking round in a daze. Overcome with emotion and tiredness and have only just entered our second week of introductions. I manage to prepare and cook a proper meal for us but leave the washing up until the next morning.

My husband is starting to wonder why the introductions seem to be taking so long; he just wants our children to be with us so that we can start living as a family. *Today we did no miles.*

Wed 28th April

We leave home at 11.45am, and at 1.00pm we collect Julie from school, after spending a little time with Julie we go to the foster home. It's wet weather again and so we stay indoors. We put the children to bed at 7.00 and arrive home at 8.15pm. *Today we travelled 86 miles.*

Thu 29th April

We leave home at 8.45am, as today we have to attend a mid-way review meeting with the foster carers, Sarah, Anna and Marty, which starts at 10.00am. We all seem to think that everything is going ok and we all agree that there need to be no changes to the rest of the introduction plans. At 1.00pm we collect Julie from school, it's her last day at her old school and the other pupils make a fuss of saying good-bye. They have all drawn a miniature picture of themselves and stuck it to a giant good-bye card. On the way there we collected James from the babysitter's home, ready prepared with a bag containing nightclothes. That afternoon we visited my parent's house, and then called at Lucy's house. We arrived home, had some tea with the children, bathed them, got them ready for bed and set off in the car to take them home. Time management kind of went out of the window and I had to phone ahead to say that we were going to be late. We arrived at the foster home at 7.15pm, put the children to bed and left to come back home. We arrived home at 8.45pm. *Today we travelled 152 miles.*

Fri 30th April

Today Anna brought James and Julie to our home, and dropped them off at 10.30am. We had a cup of tea and a short conversation and then she left, leaving the children with us. They played in the garden and my husband told Julie that their first project together was to complete the garden pond and put some fish in it. After lunch we took them to Julie's new school so she could meet the other children and her new teacher. We completed various bits of paper and purchased some polo shirts with the school logo embroidered on them. After tea we took the children back to the foster home and put them to bed. By now we had taken most of their clothes and toys to our house. *Today we travelled 79 miles.*

Sat 1st May

We leave home at 8.15am and arrive to collect our children at 9.30am. We take them back to our house and after a quick cup of tea we set off on a shopping trip. We buy foods like dinosaurs and jetters and oven chips as well as petit filous yoghurts, orange squash and chicken dippers. Then we call at another shopping centre and purchase Julie's new school clothes, skirts, shirts, cardigans, plimsolls, etc. After tea we take the children back to the foster home and kiss them goodnight in someone else's home for the last time. *Today we travelled 158 miles.*

Sun 2nd May

This was our rest day, and the last day that the foster carers would have our children to themselves. It's a day for them to say their goodbyes. For us this day dragged. We had been told that when we collected our children it would need to be an in-and-out visit. Literally call at the door, get the children and the last of their belongings, get in the car and go. Now I know why. Today the car did not move.

Mon 3rd May

PLACEMENT DAY!. Today we collect our children for the last time. We leave home at 7.45am and arrive at the foster home at 9.00am. The children are ready. We have taken along a card and some flowers as a thank you and I hand them over as soon as the door is opened. James has filled his nappy so I change him while my husband and the foster dad put the children's last few items in our car. Then we are ready. We get to the door and that's where we lose it emotionally. The foster carers have made sure that their own grown-up children are around to say good-bye and we all hug. We walk down their garden path to the car and the foster mum hands me a carrier bag with a gift each for the children and a card for us. None of us can bring ourselves to say anything; we are all teary eyed, except for the children who are embarking on a great adventure. The foster carers give Julie one last hug and she gets into our car. Ray fastens her seat belt as the foster dad picks up James to say good-bye. For one brief moment I look at the foster dad's flushed face and can only think that he is about to run back into the house with my son, lock the door and not come out. But he doesn't. My husband can't take anymore; he gets into our car and leaves me to put our son in his car seat next to our daughter. I get in the front seat and manage to blurt out a "Thanks, bye," and my husband pulls away from the kerb. I cry practically all the way home. I feel like I am stealing these children. This should be the happiest day of my life and yet I am blubbering like a baby. Even now, months later as I sit at my computer at ten past eleven at night writing this with my children tucked up in bed and my husband snoring, tears are dripping down my cheeks thinking of the day we collected our children. *Today we travelled 79 Miles.*

Right from this day, our children called us Mummy and Daddy. After so long waiting and hoping for a family, someone was calling me Mummy. By the third day we had had a trip to the hairdressers where James had his 'girly curls' cut off. It changed him so much and he now looks like a typical little boy.

The first few days that our children were with us seemed to fly by, not only were we tired out from the previous fortnight's travelling, but we now had two young children to look after too. As we wanted to try and keep at least some routine going,

Julie started at her new school the very next day, Tuesday 4th May. My husband had gone back to work so it was up to me to sort the breakfast and school run. At 8.30 we were ready to roll, I got the camera out and took a photo of Julie in her new uniform - for the family book - got us all in coats and shoes and set off walking. At the school gates I got my mobile out and phoned my husband, then passed the phone to Julie, he wished her luck and told her she could tell him all about it when he got home from work. My husband had arranged to change his working hours for the first few months to 7am until 4pm so that he would have the chance to eat tea with us all as a family.

After Julie had given me the phone back, we went into school. Not quite knowing where to go I took the children though the main entrance and into the dining area where the breakfast club was in full swing, after a quick glance round I managed to find a teacher that I knew and headed in her direction. After a quick hello, I kissed Julie goodbye and told her not to worry and that I would be there to pick her up that afternoon. I left her in her teacher's capable hands and turned to walk away. James was in his pram and before I could even get out of the building I could feel tears burning my eyes. I could not believe how strongly I felt for the child I had just dropped off at a new strange school full of strange people after only knowing her for two weeks and having only spent one day in our home.

The first couple of nights I was woken by Julie standing at the side of our bed. The first time she got in with us. My husband and I ended up teetering on the edges of the mattress and when I woke first the following morning I was surprised - and shocked - to find Julie had taken her pyjama top off and was complaining that she was hot. I am not sure why I was shocked, it was just something that was totally unexpected, something I had not had to deal with before. The next night I took her back to her own bed, settled her down and returned to my bed. I had decided a long time ago that regardless of what my children had been through - to a certain extent - my husband and I were going to be firm but fair from the start, and not turn into 'doormats'. It may sound heartless but we needed our children to feel safe and ok from the start.

On 7th May Anna arrived on her first statutory visit since the children had been placed with us. She arrived at two in the afternoon and after a cup of tea and a chat, the three of us walked to school to collect Julie. After we got home I took James into the living room and left Anna and Julie alone in the dining room. After an hour Anna and I had another chat and she left. Both the children seemed to be settling in quite well. Julie had obvious questions about the foster carers, but other than that had begun to accept the situation. She loved her new room, but was a little concerned about sleeping in there on her own.

On 13th May Sarah - our social worker - came to see us in the morning followed by Anna in the afternoon. By this time we had started to change the old routines and instill some of our own. The children still went to bed at seven, but instead of just James having a bedtime Horlicks drink, they both had one, and instead of Julie going to bed first, they went to bed at the same time.

On 17th May we left our children for the first time, in the hands of my mother. She arrived at 5.30 and at quarter to six we left to attend our first support meeting. I called home to see if things were ok and we arrived home at quarter past ten to reports that the children had been fine. We went upstairs, kissed our sleeping angels goodnight and after mother left, we went to bed.

Not long after, the bed wetting started and things seemed to go a little downhill with Julie. My husband and I were getting frustrated, and being a little short with each other as well as with our children, then we began to worry that this would lead to all sorts of problems. Having spoken to Anna a few times she made a date to come and see me and my husband whilst Julie was at school so that we could talk about all the things we felt were problematic, but before that, we had our first review to get through.

This took place at our house on 21st May. That morning I had taken all the relevant paperwork, and James, and registered the children with our family doctor. At 2pm that afternoon, Anna arrived with the Independent Reviewing officer, and Trevor arrived in place of Sarah who was on holiday. I had arranged for my parents to collect Julie from school and when they arrived they took both the children out to play in the garden. This gave us a chance to focus on the review knowing that our children were safe in the garden with their grandparents. It was also nice for the reviewing officer, and social workers to see that the children had settled and were bonding well with their grandparents and vice versa.

Anna came to see Ray and I the following Monday morning at 9.30 after I had dropped Julie at school. We talked about a lot of issues. It transpired that not only were we expecting too much of our children, but we were also expecting too much of ourselves. Anna's best advice was to take a step back and re-evaluate the situation - in her eyes we were doing great, everything was fine. We just needed to hear that. After all, we were at that time 'new parents'. We took her advice and things got back on track. To tackle the bed-wetting we began getting Julie up between 10.30 and 11.30 at night, as we were on our way to bed. It seems to have worked, we still do it now and in the past five months we have only had two wet beds.

Anna carried on her visits, working in hourly sessions with Julie about once every two weeks, after which Anna and I discussed the session and any related news that she had for us. We also made sure that Anna knew everything that had happened, be it good or bad and sometimes I would start to tell her things as soon as she got in the door. I can honestly say that this helped tremendously as Anna was able to offer us help and advice and sometimes steer us in the right direction. As you can understand, if she does not know about it, she can't do anything about it.

Sometimes I wondered if there were things I should not have said, but came to the conclusion that telling her everything - good and bad - was better for everyone concerned. As the saying goes, 'it'll all come out in the wash anyway.'

On 10th June Anna arrived at 2 and we went to collect Julie from school. Julie, James and I set off back home and Anna stayed behind and met with the teacher to prepare Julie's Personal Education Plan. This turned out to be so different from the one done at her last school that it is almost like reading PEP's for two different people. Reading her PEP for her old school was like reading a report of a troubled child, she was quiet, and although she had a lot of friends, was quite content to be on her own. Her new one was quite the opposite!

From the start of the introductions, the plan has been to move at a pace that the children can feel comfortable with. Part of this process involves giving the children time and space, not only to welcome new parents and a whole new life, but also to allow them time to grieve for the loss of foster carers, particularly important when the children are at an age such as Julie's. James is just James. As long as he is fed and watered and loved then he is happy. But with Julie there are always questions and issues that need addressing truthfully and honestly, even if the answer is 'I don't know' or the subject is perhaps not something that you yourself are comfortable with. There was the incident where Julie did tell her dad that she didn't want to live with us, that she wanted to go back to the foster carers because they let her have chocolate spread on toast. My husband, who at the time was doing woodwork in the garden and was rather exhausted, simply said, "Ok, go pack a bag and I will drive you over." I must stress that we have never and will never use this as a threat to either of our children but as an answer to her request it made her realise that we were not pushovers. Yes our children are special and mean the earth to us but we were determined not to pander to every little whim, begging them for love and trust by giving into their every desire. Later that afternoon, when Julie had come back in the house and was sat at the table colouring, my husband enquired as to whether she was ready to go. "No," she replied, "I have decided to stay here, even if I can't have chocolate spread."

As part of the 'letting go' process, Anna suggested letting the children speak on the phone to the foster carers. We were all for it, anything to help Julie along was a good idea to us. I knew that the foster carers had since had some more children placed with them so I phoned a couple of days in advance to arrange the call. The following Monday I was washing the tea pots in the kitchen, Ray was still at the table by the side of James in his high chair. I dried my hands, picked up the cordless and dialled the number. After a quick "Hello," I passed the phone over to Julie. She hovered about in the hall and after a few minutes of conversation took the phone into the dining room, held the phone to James's face and said "James, talk to mum, on the phone."

James' response was to shuffle in his chair trying to locate me in the kitchen. He took the phone and spoke a few words. My husband came into the kitchen in utter disbelief at what he had just heard. At first, I was ok with it, but by the time we spoke to Anna I was the one who was extremely upset and my husband was the one who was ok with it. The reason it was so upsetting to hear, was because Julie and James had never called their foster carers Mum and Dad. They had always called them by their first names.

After the first few weeks of having our children with us, we felt that things had started to go downhill. Julie began wetting the bed at night and didn't seem to be trying hard enough with her schoolwork. We were starting to get angry at each other and were having arguments after the children had gone to bed. I talked to Anna about this and she arranged to come and see us one night after the children were asleep. Anna was brilliant. It's so nice to be able to talk to someone who, whilst knowing all the background information about the children, is also a step outside the family and can help you to take a step out and look in on the situation. Not only were we expecting too much of our children, but we were expecting too much of ourselves. We talked about how we use our voices, and how children learn and grow at different rates. Anna also found us some information as a very basic guideline to help us understand what kind of things children could be doing by what age. What we also found was that because Julie is so tall, you look at her and automatically think that she is a seven or eight year old, not five. This talk with Anna really helped us to put things into perspective, and to change things accordingly, and it helped. We solved the bed-wetting by getting her up to go to the toilet when we went up to bed. Once Julie is awake in the morning, she will happily take herself off to the toilet and get back in bed until I go in to get her up, but she just could not wake herself in the middle of the night until it was too late. We now get her up at half past ten. On average, twice a week my husband and I will be watching the television when at exactly 27 minutes past ten we will hear her flush the toilet. We are getting there.

On 14th June we all took a trip to the dentist. We registered the children, I had a filling, my husband had his teeth cleaned and both Julie and James had their teeth checked. We had to make another appointment for Julie to have two fillings. That, I was not looking forward to!

My husband and I also had appointments with the opticians, so we booked Julie in too. She now has to wear glasses when reading/writing etc. as it turns out she is long sighted.

A few days later we had a shopping trip and started buying the children new clothes. Jeans, vests, t-shirts, shoes and the like filled our trolley. It was brilliant! Asda's George range for kids is great, and not too expensive. The only minor problem I have is that Julie is quite tall. She is five years old but depending where I shop, I have to buy clothes that are labelled for 8 to 9 year olds. This makes it a little difficult if I am out shopping with James while Julie is at school, I have to think twice before buying so I try to wait until the weekend when I can take her with me.

Back at the dentist Julie had her two fillings. Being the kind of person that 'tells it like it is' I talked to Julie about what was going to happen and the fact that yes it would hurt, but it would be over quickly and that I would be there in the room holding her hand. How wrong was I! No sooner had she sat in the chair, the dentist filled the bad teeth, no drilling, and said "Ok, that's it." The dental nurse gave Julie two stickers and before I knew it we were back in the car. Boy, have things changed since I was 16! Needless to say, the journey home consisted of Julie saying "I was very brave wasn't I, Mum, it didn't hurt at all."

On Father's Day we took our first outing to the seaside. We could not believe how well behaved our children were! They did not pester for anything, they did not run off causing havoc, they held our hands when walking and they were impeccable in the café, and to top off a great day, they fell asleep in the car on the way home!

On 21st June we had our first visit from the Health Visitor. She came and looked through James's health record and asked me a few questions, then turned her attention to James. The Health Visitor had brought a box with her containing a mixture of small toys which

James had gotten into straight away, she picked up a couple of toys and asked him what they were, which he answered correctly. Next she asked him to find a small wooden toy table and chair, which he did, then she asked him to stack as many small wooden blocks onto the toy table as he could without them falling over. As this was his 18 to 24 month check, the health visitor was expecting him to stack four blocks on the toy table. James stacked six before knocking them over himself.

On 22nd June our social worker Sarah came to visit us. By this time she had begun to arrive around 7.15 in the evening as by that time the children were in bed asleep which meant that we could sit and focus all our attentions on the matters in hand. We discussed changing the children's middle names and talked about meeting their birth mother. We were very unsure about this but over the coming months, and after much discussion with both Sarah and Anna, we decided that this would be a good idea. However, knowing the children's birth mothers' knack of not always turning up for appointments, and the fact that the whole thing would be very trying on Ray's and my emotions, we decided that there would only be one chance for this meeting to happen, and if the children's birth mother did not turn up for the appointment, then another time would not be arranged. We also discussed security of the matter. The children had been adopted out of their birth area for a reason, and so it was decided that on the day of the meeting we would get together with Sarah half way there, and travel in her car the rest of the way. So now we wait until that meeting is arranged.

14

At the beginning of July James turned two and we decided to have a little birthday party for him. Lots of family and friends came and we played various party games and ate lots of typical party food and sweets. I'm not exactly sure what he thought of the party, but once we had got him opening presents he seemed to get into the spirit. He was particularly pleased with the extra-large water pistol that Uncle Bill and Auntie Sophie had bought for him! And all the children enjoyed playing in the sand pit that Nana and Granddad had bought. Julie also received small gifts from most people that came, a sort of 'welcome to the family, you will not be left out' kind of gesture. At one point, Julie took hold of the hand of my husband's friend's wife and whisked her upstairs to show her, her 'new' bedroom, where she said to her, "My mum makes the best party food ever." And on the way back down remarked, "Why do people keep giving me presents, it's James' birthday?"

By this time we had started to think about a holiday. I was happy to stay at home but my husband insisted that we go away - just for a week to see how the children would be. After surfing the Internet for a couple of hours while Julie was at school and James was napping, I had booked us a week in a caravan at a beachside site in North Wales. All was set for 24th July.

The weeks leading up to the holiday were filled with shopping for new shorts and t-shirts and a new swimming costume. Julie already had a bikini but personally I don't like to see young girls in bikinis. Don't ask me why, I just don't like it. I managed to find two lovely costumes, one a lovely lilac colour with sparkly bits and a pink one - Julie's favourite colour. We also purchased a pair of trunks for James which have towelling inside and a waterproof layer between that and the outside pattern, just in case. Up to now they've not been needed, apart from when I took him to the local pool, got him ready and then stood him on the changing room bench whilst I changed, at which time he decided to take a pee!

We also decided to make a list of all the things we would need to take with us. Such things as the travel cot, high chair, push chair, plates, cutlery and bibs, wipes and nappies, things that were 'out of the norm'. Incidentally, we never used the pushchair on that holiday, although all four of us ended up with blisters on our feet.

On Anna's next visit we talked about
meeting up with the foster parents. After the
phone call incident I was very unhappy
about having to take my children to meet the
foster carers. I tried to make excuses and at
one point I thought Anna was getting a little
bit miffed that I was trying so hard to get out
of it. I had visions of getting out of the car
and my children running into the arms of the
foster carers without a second thought for us,
although the one good thing that Anna did
assure me of was that we did not have to
take our children back to the old foster home,

as when these visits were made, they were usually done in a public place like a park or playing area. That put my mind at ease a little, and also the fact that Anna was determined to prove to me that the children had made attachments with us and would not, as I put it, go 'running off into their foster carers arms with no thoughts whatsoever of us'.

Due to holidays and various shift patterns that the foster carers were working, we made arrangements to meet up at a local park on our return from Wales. That suited me down to the ground. The last thing I wanted was to go on holiday in a caravan with two children whose world had been totally turned upside down by a meeting with their foster carers.

We left our hometown and headed for Wales on 24th July. As we were towing a trailer we had to keep to a speed limit of 50 mph, so the journey took us the best part of four and a half hours. Thank the Lord for air-conditioning. The journey wasn't exactly a nightmare, just different with constant bickering and questioning coming from the back seat, not to mention cries of "are we there yet?" And as for story tapes, by the time we got to the Elves and the Shoemaker we were telling the children to be quiet because we couldn't hear the story! Halfway through the journey we found a rest stop, visited the toilets, changed James's nappy and had a bite to eat. Needless to say the next two hours were fantastic. The children fell asleep before we got back onto the motorway and we turned over to radio 2. Heaven.

The holiday itself was a lot better than we had anticipated. There were a few down moments, but these happen just as much in a 'birth' family. We spent evenings walking up and down the beach with nets and buckets trying to catch things from rock pools. We did manage to catch a couple of crabs in a rather embarrassing sexual hold, which we passed off as 'hugging' and had a good laugh about later. The children really enjoyed the site club too, there was always something on for the children, and at times we had difficulty keeping tabs on them both, even James wanted to be bopping on the dance floor rather than sat at a table with a bottle of fruit shoot and packet of quavers. We also met some lovely people there who came from mid-Wales. They have three children, two of which were on holiday with them, and who were Julie's age, I really think that they helped to bring Julie out of her shell as on our return she seemed a lot more confident in herself.

We spent our last night in the site club with our new friends, swapped numbers and addresses and said we would keep in touch. Days after returning home my new friend phoned, two hours later we hung up and have been like it ever since.

We came home on 31st July and arranged the meeting with the foster carers for the 2nd August. As we knew they had had some more children placed with them, we asked if they could come along too, seeing that the foster carers had moved on might make it easier for Julie to move on too.

That morning we got ready. I still had not quite got the hang of children and time management, so at the last minute I was dashing around upstairs getting the children's clothes ready for my husband to get them dressed. For some reason I was determined to make sure that both James and Julie were dressed from head to foot in something that I had bought for them, even down to socks shoes and knickers. I am not quite sure why I did this, but it made me feel good. There will be an explanation somewhere along the lines. And so we set off.

As we were not quite sure where we were going, we met up in the car park of a local fast food restaurant and followed the foster carers to a local park, paid our entry fee, and parked the car. I took one last sorrowful glance at my husband, said, "Here goes everything," and opened the car door. The foster carers were busy getting their new children out of their car as we opened our back doors for James and Julie to get out. As they did, the foster carers beamed and called "Hello there, remember us?" To my complete and utter astonishment, Julie said a quick and quiet "Hello," under her breath, and James hid behind Ray's legs and would not budge until my husband explained that these people were not strangers and that James could come out and say hello. Once the formalities were over, we headed over to the play park, found a bench and began to chat just like old friends as the children went and played.

We sat there for what seemed like ages; in fact it was probably about two hours before we all decided that it was time to get back. The foster carers were getting ready to go on their holiday a couple of days later and were in the middle of packing. We walked back to the car and said our good-byes. One of the last things that the foster carers said to us as we got in the car was, "Those children are a credit to you both, well done."

I couldn't wait for Anna's next appointment so that I could tell her how good the visit had been.

Things from then on started to settle down. Anna continued to call on a regular basis but didn't seem to be doing as much intensive work with Julie. Both she and Sarah were surprised and happy at the rate at which the children were settling with us.

At the end of August my parents decided to spend the bank holiday weekend at their holiday home and asked if they could take the children with them. I cleared this with Anna and began making preparations. My husband and I saw this as a good opportunity to visit our friends in Wales who we had met on holiday a few months earlier, and after a week of packing and research into B&B's we dropped the children off with their luggage. We didn't stay long, the children were not clingy, but as we said goodbye James hugged his dad and said "Don't go dad." Then he turned and ran off into the living room and we left. Determined not to be 'over anxious' I didn't phone to check on them until we got to our first rest stop. I spoke to my mother who assured me that the children were fine. I did not speak to them, as, being a little upset at leaving them; I did not want to upset the children. We carried on our way and arrived at our friend's house a couple of hours earlier than we expected. After a cup of tea and chat our friends took us to the B&B and we unpacked, then we went back for drinks and supper, finally crawling to our beds at midnight. We slept like logs and enjoyed getting up in a leisurely way with a full English breakfast waiting for us and no pots to wash or children to get ready. The second night, however, was worse. I woke at 2 in the morning having had a nightmare that something had happened and our children had been taken away from us. As I reached out for my husband I forgot that we were in twin beds with a bedside table between us and promptly sent the table lamp flying which in turn rattled my husband's coffee cup from the night before, waking him up. Once settled, I decided that the following morning I would call straight after breakfast to make sure all was ok. I did call only to find that the children had taken the dog for a walk with my step father so that mother could have a shower in peace.

We travelled back on the Tuesday morning so that my husband could call into work on the afternoon, and just after lunchtime my mother and step father arrived with our children, and what looked like twice as much luggage as they left with. Seven loads later, the laundry was done!

They had had a wonderful time and were full of stories about visiting friends and meeting other children, walks on the beach and pub Sunday dinners. But mother looked dead tired! Later that afternoon I phoned to see if she'd enjoyed it, only to be told by my step father that mother had got on the settee for an hours sleep, even before tackling their laundry - something she would never normally do.

By the time September came round, our adoption application paperwork had been sorted out, and arrangements made for the children's adoption medicals to be done by our local Doctor. Everything seemed ok, although he commented that Julie was a little overweight for her age. I resisted the temptation to say that Julie was the height of a 7/8 year old and had actually lost pounds since being placed. Instead I decided that if the social workers were happy, then that was fine for me.

About this time I noticed that some of my

jeans were not as tight as they used to be. I found that within the first six months of having my children placed with me, I had actually dropped two dress sizes. Other people started to notice too.

By this time my six months statutory adoption leave from work was just about up. I visited a couple of times but suitable hours could not be worked out. I had wanted to work on a part time basis so that I could drop off and collect Julie from school myself. After all, my husband and I had not spent two years getting our children so that we could hand them over to a child-minder to bring them up whilst we went out to work full time! My employer and I came to a compromise agreement, and on 10th October I finished work.

After a while I began to feel quite uneasy about being unemployed. I had looked into childcare so that I could work four days a week 10 until 2, this would mean putting James in a crèche or with a registered child-minder from 9.30 until 2.30 which on average would cost me £60.00 a week. Who would pay me £60.00 a week (after deductions and travelling expenses) for 16 hours work, not to mention that in the school holidays the childcare bill would rise to an average of £120.00 for 2 children. Also, based on that fact that my husband works full time, we are not entitled to any extra Child/Working Tax Credits or help with childcare costs. I must admit, with Julie's birthday and Christmas coming up I was a little on the worried side. Not wanting to burden our children with this, we talked about it at night. After one particular discussion with my husband, I ranted on that I was no longer contributing anything to our home, that I was useless, and as thick as two short planks stuck together with crazy glue, I must be as this was how I felt I was looked upon every time I went into the Job Centre, as if I was begging. My husband assured me that I was not thick and convinced me that I was putting a lot more into our home than I thought, after all, he leaves for work at 6 in the morning and is sometimes not home until after six in the evening and so I am keeping the house and the children - in itself a massively understated job. This made me feel a lot better about myself, and also less guilty about spending time and effort on my family and not handing them over while I go in search of that perfect career. I guess for me it is so nice to be able to collect Julie from school, watch her do homework, help her read, and feed my children a proper healthy 'sit at a table' meal rather than rush home from the child-minders', bang in a frozen pizza and pack them off to bed without so much as a 'what have you done today?' talk. Being a stay at home mum may not be for everyone though. I think it's very much a personal decision, but not one to take lightly. I also think that my children have positively benefited from the fact that I am always there for them. They have had such a pillar to post start that the last thing I wanted to be was a part time mum.

18

Julie's birthday was on the horizon. She had mentioned something about having a party as a couple of her friends had had parties at the nearby Wacky Warehouse. We talked to her about having a Halloween party a week after her birthday and she said that would be good. We decorated the whole of the downstairs of the house with fake cobwebs, spiders, skeletons, bats, ghosts and witches, you name it we had it. We even had special tape on the windows that said CAUTION, HAUNTED HOUSE DO NOT ENTER. I had bought some little prizes for the games and spent three days wrapping gifts for pass the parcel. I even hollowed out a proper pumpkin and gave the mush to Uncle Bill to make a traditional American pumpkin pie. The party was a great success, Julie was dressed as a witch, and James was dressed as Dracula, complete with spiky hair and his dad's black bow tie.

Christmas was, by this time, fast approaching and on 27th November we put up the Christmas decorations, complete with new ones including a musical polar bear and snowman. We did at least seven shopping trips without the children and wrapped and hid presents in various cupboards. Quite a few presents had to be stored at my parent's house as we quickly ran out of room.

Of course the children knew it was Christmastime and that Santa would be visiting. As we don't have a fireplace or chimney, we told the children that Santa had a magic key that would let him into the house but that he wasn't able to come upstairs or go into the children's bedrooms. We didn't actually tell the children when it was Christmas Eve, my husband and I had discussed this and decided that we would have enough to do without Julie and James running about all night looking out of the window watching for flying reindeer.

When we took the children to bed that night, I mentioned to James that if he went straight to sleep, that maybe Santa would visit. He just looked at me as if to say 'what planet are you on mum?' Julie had already guessed that it was Christmas Eve as it had been mentioned on the television so many times earlier that evening, so when I tucked her in I told her that, although it was Christmas Eve, Santa would not leave any presents if she were to stay awake, and that in the morning she must stay in bed until we went in to fetch her.

Once they were settled and asleep, I drove over to my parents to fetch all the presents. When I got back we emptied all the cupboards and began setting everything out. We couldn't believe how much we had amassed. The presents half covered the living room floor and completely covered the conservatory floor. We topped of the look by sprinkling white glitter on the room and hall carpet to look like Santa's footprints. The place looked magical.

All our friends and family had said that we were mad, and that regardless of what we did or said, the children would be up at 5am looking to see if Santa had been. Nothing could be further from the truth.

I had bought a camcorder for Ray for Christmas, and was determined not to be caught on camera in my pyjamas so I got up at 6.30am, quickly showered, dressed and put on make-up. James was still fast asleep and Julie had done what she does every morning, been to the toilet and then got back in bed. At quarter past seven, I went downstairs and got the camcorder ready while my husband got the children out of bed, put on their dressing gowns and came downstairs. As I sat there I could hear them talking about the footprints, and how mum would be hoovering up all day! As they came into the room they stood for a few seconds looking at all the gifts, and slowly began to pick out which were theirs. One big mistake we made was to just put the presents all over, next year we will separate them into piles-per-person, as my husband spent an hour or so picking each present up and reading the tags to make sure that the children were not opening someone else's gift.

The first present James opened was a 'Bob the Builder' playset. Once opened he was not interested in anything else, he just kept asking, "Can I have it?" I tried to explain that he had to open the rest of his presents first, but in the end I had to take the playset away until he had opened the rest of his gifts, by which time he had forgotten about it and was playing with his new set of cars.

Later that day, Lucy and Adrian and my mother and step father arrived which resulted in another load of gifts coming through the front door to be opened, and then, after a traditional Christmas dinner of salmon, prawns, turkey, beef, pork, new potatoes, roast potatoes, peas, carrots, broccoli, savoy cabbage, stuffing, pigs in blankets, gravy and strawberry and cream shortcake, we retired back to the living room to start unpacking toys from their boxes and fixing things together. I think next year we might unpack and fix everything the night before as on more than one occasion I had to rescue bits of boxes from the rubbish bags destined for the local tip so that I could see how various toy sets fitted together!

Even though we all had bouts of sickness and diarrhoea, James' was the worst, with a trip to the emergency doctor, we had the best Christmas ever.

January and school came all too quickly, but I think we were all glad to get back to a 'normal' routine.

By this time, Anna had told us that she had
had contact with the children's birth mother,
and that, whilst she was willing to consent to
the adoption, she could not say the same for
James's birth father. She did think that she
could convince him that it would be for the
best but could not be 100%. With this in
mind, we all thought that the legalities of the
adoption would be done and dusted by
March time; as, if consent was given, it
would just be a case of the courts taking
away the birth parents' parental
responsibility for the children and giving it to

us. However, it was becoming increasingly clear that that was perhaps not to be the case. The birth parents had missed appointments with Anna, and she was finding it difficult to track them down. I was getting a little impatient at this because as far as I was concerned, they had had all the chances that they deserved. On the 1st February we had our third review with the independent reviewing officer, Anna, Sarah and me. Due to work commitments, my husband was unable to be there, this, however, did not cause any problems.

Among other things, we talked about Anna having difficulty tracking down the children's birth parents, as it seemed as if they were constantly on the move. By this point Anna had discussed with her manager the scenarios of moving forward with the application to court, and had decided that this would be brought up at the review so that a definite decision could be made.

Not knowing this, I said that I thought it was time to admit that the chance of getting the birth parents' consent was practically non-existent and that we should forge ahead and go to court to ask them to dispense with the birth parents' consent. At this point I had to leave the room to chase after James who had decided to go upstairs. When I returned to the room, everyone had decided that we were to forge ahead without consent. The only problem was that this could put quite a few months onto the process. Hopefully, the legal side would be completed before Christmas 2005.

For the first part of the year, things were going great. We did have bad days, but doesn't everyone?

20

Julie was by now, on her third pair of glasses, although her eyes are getting better, and she does not need to go back for 12 months. She has also lost three teeth, had a broken one removed and is due back at the dentist in a few weeks to have a bad one out. Her reading and writing have improved tenfold, and we are very proud of her achievements in school. She has turned from a shy girl into a regular, well-liked member of her class, and most days when I pick her up she has a big smile for me.

Her bedwetting had practically stopped.

We still got her out of bed to go to the toilet at 10.30pm, but now, there are at least three nights a week that she actually gets herself out of bed, goes to the toilet, and then goes back to bed. We have even managed to get her to wipe herself properly and flush the loo after she has been, although I still don't seem to be able to get her to remember to shut the bathroom door when she is in there.

James, well he is just James. Typical daredevil! We are getting through the 'terrible twos' with only small scars, and what he lacks in potty training, he certainly makes up for in everything else. His favourite songs, that he sings, are Twinkle Twinkle Little Star, Hey Baby, 1,2,3,4,5 Once I Caught a Fish Alive and Strawberry Fields Forever. You can hold a perfect conversation with him and he knows plenty of colours, including silver, white and purple.

He recently decided that he would start climbing out of his cot in the early mornings, to play with his toys or look out of the window, so my husband and I decided that it might be a good idea to take one of the sides off his cot. We do have a baby gate on his bedroom door so it's not as if he can get up and go walkabout in the night. He now thinks that he has a big boy bed, complete with pillow, and rushes upstairs at bedtime to jump in. The third night we did this, we went up to check and found that he was asleep on the floor! Luckily, he is only a few inches off the floor so he didn't hurt himself, in fact, from the way he was laid; I don't even think he woke himself up!

We are living as a normal family, getting on with whatever life throws at us. No two days are ever the same.

21

We seemed to spend a lifetime waiting for the relevant papers to be brought out to us so that we could sign to lodge adoption papers with the court. Because we were planning to adopt without the birth parents consent we had to wait until a Guardian was appointed. No one was sure how long this would take, but we had high hopes of having everything completed by the summer. We had already decided that we would like to have both children christened after the legalities are completed, and had therefore decided who would be Godparents. That is something I was very much looking forward to, as to me it would signify the end of a very long journey.

But for that moment, I had to hold myself back and put all my energies into preparing for court, and any problems that may have arisen. Until then, we went on living life as a 'normal' family, getting on with the things that families do. School runs, Doctors, Dentists, friends, shower nights, cartoons and hoovering every day.

At the end of January, my husband and I were sat at the dining table one Saturday morning reading the papers. I had the local paper and was shuffling through the properties for sale, not that we were thinking of moving, but after being in our house for five years, and having done so much to it, I was interested to see what, as an approximation, it would now be worth. Quite a few houses I looked at were roughly the same as ours, except some would have a downstairs toilet or an en-suite. At that time, we only had one toilet, and that was in the family bathroom. "What we need," I suddenly said to Ray, "Is an en-suite." He choked on his cup of tea and asked me what planet I was on.

After half an hour I had managed to turn the conversation around to make him think that it was his idea, and had sent him across the road to talk to our neighbour who happened to be a plumber. A week later we had started work. We totally ripped out our bedroom, bare walls, floor the lot and began. We had some new wardrobes given to us by a family friend and scoured everywhere for basic cheap, but decent, pottery. What we ended up with was a totally new bedroom complete with an en-suite that included a full size sink, toilet and shower cubicle. I have to say, it's a godsend. We now have two toilets, great for family and guests! And it only took us 10 weeks to complete.

Easter quickly followed, as too did an appointment for the children to have their next statutory medical. At James' I discussed potty training with the Doctor who felt that now would be a good time as at nearly 33 months old, James' urine would now be getting stronger and would start to smell, meaning that I would have to wash him every morning and night. We talked about how I was going to do it, and I decided that Easter would be a good time to start.

My husband and I rarely travel anywhere during the bank holidays as there is always a build-up of traffic, a couple of years previous we had been stuck in a traffic jam for four hours on a journey to our local video store that would normally have taken ten minutes, since then we had preferred to stay at home.

I knew that we would be having a couple of days at home with no shopping trips planned so one Thursday morning I dressed James in a t-shirt, socks and pants, and brought his potty downstairs.

James had sat on both the potty and the toilet in the past, so was used to it, but had never really got into actually telling us that he needed to go. I thought I was in for a rough ride. That day, we went through seven pairs of pants.

Most of the time, James had only let a little urine leak out before rushing into the kitchen to get on the potty, and after the first accident he asked to have a nappy back on. I told him "no," that we would persevere. A few days later we were taking short trips to the shop and park, and after eight days he was potty trained. We still continued to have the potty downstairs, and he still wears nappies for bed, but during the day he is dry.

A couple of weeks after this, we found out that James suffers from eczema. A trip to the doctors confirmed this, and he prescribed lotion for James' bath and cream to rub on afterwards. He is now a lot better, although I am looking out for other symptoms that usually go hand in hand with eczema such as hay fever and asthma. Up to yet, nothing has emerged.

Julie continued to improve at school beyond all expectations, and after an initial growing spurt is now wearing clothes that are more her age range. She has lost quite a lot of weight and enjoys a varied lifestyle with much more sport input. She really enjoys PE at school and even goes to the after school clubs for sport activities and football.

By the end of April, our social worker Sarah had arranged to see us and brought us the relevant paperwork for the legal side of the adoption. As we are adopting two children, there were two lots of paperwork, each lot having three copies, which we had to read, check and sign. We spent a couple of hours with Sarah doing this, added the children's birth certificates and sent them off recorded delivery to the court. We now had to wait for a reply, after which a Guardian would be appointed.

A couple of months later we got a reply telling us that a Directions hearing had been scheduled for July. We would not be able to attend this hearing, but the social workers and guardian would be there to map out the coming months in terms of who would be doing what, and when it had to be done by. Around the same time as we got this information, we also had a phone call from Anna who had managed to not only track down the birth parents, but had also arranged a meeting with them both to talk about consenting to the adoption and arranging for us to meet them.

A couple of days later Anna called to say that a meeting had been arranged and that the birth parents had not only seen the guardian but had also signed the consent forms!

The birth parents had accepted that they

could not look after the children properly. They accepted that no matter what they did, there was no way after such a long time, that they would ever get the children back, and not only that, they were still sorting themselves out and did not know how long it would take. But they wanted to meet us, and so we agreed.

Sarah came out to see us just before the meeting to go over a few things and ask how we were feeling about seeing the birth parents. As I told her, part of me wanted to go in there and, to put it bluntly, rip their heads off, how can anyone treat their children the way they did? But the other half of me felt quite thankful, after all, if they had not done what they did, then I would not be a mother.

The meeting was arranged. We met up with Sarah at the adoption offices and she then drove us to the family centre where a room had been booked for us. We got a cup of tea and settled down. Ten minutes later they came in with Anna. It was like looking at two six-foot versions of our children.

We had gone into that meeting expecting these people to be quite cocky and angry, they in turn, had expected us to be posh, rich and judgmental towards them. Nothing could have been further from the truth, they looked, to me, as 'normal' as anyone else I know.

We had taken with us a number of photos showing how much the children had changed since they had been with us, and also a handful of pictures for the birth parents to take away with them.

We chatted for a couple of hours, telling them about what the children had been up to. The first question they asked us was, "Is James talking yet?" to which our answer was "Talking, we have difficulty shutting him up!" We told them about how the children both love running round the park, singing, and watching Scooby-Doo, and how Julie has settled into school. They told us about what Julie had been like as a baby, what her nickname was and how they had come to choose James' name. They also brought with them a scan picture of James, and were so apologetic that they had not got one of Julie. For that picture, I will be forever thankful.

We came away from that meeting feeling as if we had known our children forever, and were extremely thankful that we had gone through with it. I now know that I will be able to answer my children's questions truthfully when they are older and they ask me what they were like as babies. It also helped the birth parents to move on to the next part of their own recovery, to know that their children were with someone who was not rich, or posh, but who would love their children and bring them up as they themselves could not.

At this time, James had been attending a crèche twice a week, which he thoroughly loved. I did, however, have him registered at a local pre-school and was waiting for the phone call to say he could start. That call came a few weeks later, which meant that he would be starting pre-school in September. He was really upset when I took him to crèche for the last time, as were his crèche teachers as they had all come to love him. So I have promised to take him in for a visit when he gets a bit older.

Once again, holiday time came round, and

we decided to go back to the same place that we went to last year, only this time we had booked for two weeks, and we had booked a sea front caravan.

We have also had notification from the courts that a date had been set for the final hearing. As the birth parents have consented, there is no need for further involvement from the guardian, which means that the process will be over and done with by the end of the summer.

With everything loaded in the car, we set off on our holidays at the beginning of August 2005. The cases were crammed into the boot, rucksacks by my feet and the bedding in the back foot wells with pillows on the back seat between Julie and James. What a journey! We had borrowed a portable video machine from my husband's friend, which hung between the two front seats and plugged into the cigar lighter at the front of the car. Unfortunately, the jack for the earphones was not working, so my husband and I had to endure the sound of Bob the Builder, Pingu, Little Mermaid and Thomas the Tank Engine all the way to Wales. Needless to say, whilst we were on holiday we found an electrical shop in the town and bought a new earphone jack and two new pairs of headphones, the journey back was bliss, the silence punctured only one or twice with shouts from James of "What Julie?, I can't hear you!"

The holiday itself was brilliant. We were there for two weeks this time, and the children both seemed a little more settled. As we were right on the sea front, we had a deck attached to the caravan that we would sit on to eat our tea. Both Julie and James couldn't wait to get into the sea, and so at the earliest opportunity, we packed the beach bag, climbed down the rocks and picked a spot just at the bottom, really handy for sending my husband back up to the caravan every hour to make a cup of tea! The children loved the sea, which made a change from the holiday the year before, where it took us practically all week to get them in up to their ankles. This year they were straight in it up to their necks, which meant I was in it up to my waist! They loved it, and could not stop laughing as each wave sloshed passed them, especially when we were on our way back to the beach, and the surf would splash up their backs. We found, (much to mine and Julie's delight) a lovely fish and chip shop in the town, and would spend hours traipsing round the market, always glad to get back to the air-conditioned car. We also spent hours in the site swimming pool where James learnt to jump in and Julie learned to float on her back without her armbands, a little more practice and she will be swimming like a fish!

Whilst in Wales, we also took a trip to Mid Wales to visit the friends that we had met the previous year. We met at their house for a cuppa and then took a walk to the park before heading off to the local pub for a pub Sunday Roast. The weather that day was lovely, so sunny it burnt my shoulders whilst we were playing football on the field at the side of the play park.

Three days after we returned from holiday we were due to go to court at 10am for the final hearing. After speaking to Anna, we arranged to meet in the car park/bus station of the town we were going to at half past nine. I had logged onto the Internet and got directions to the place we were going. At 8am we set off. Ray had decided not to follow the directions I had, as he knew that there would be traffic problems on a particular section of the motorway, and as he 'kind of knew' where we were going, he headed off the way he wanted to. We got caught in road works and were re-directed, this threw us right off, and after frantic phone calls to Anna, who in turn contacted the court, we were given a little extra time. As per usual, one of the most important days of our lives and we were going to be late due to the traffic!

We finally got to the multi-storey car park and found a place to park. The ticket machines were the same format as the ones in our own home time, so at least we knew how to work them. We entered the lift and waited. It didn't move, then it juddered, then it flew down to the ground floor with such a whoosh that I nearly fell over when it stopped. I had enough knots in my stomach without that too! After another phone call to Anna and madly waving at her from across three roads and the entrance to the bus station, we finally got together and headed to the court, which luckily, was right in front of us. We met up with Trevor who was filling in for Sarah and headed into the building. Inside we had to empty our pockets and go through the security gates. Julie and James found this highly amusing as Anna set the alarms off. We stopped off at the toilet and then went up to the courtroom where we had to wait outside.

After a short wait we were called in. The court room was nothing like what I expected. Although it was large, it was crammed full of tables with cinema style folding seats. At the front, the floor was raised to where the Judge would normally sit, but when he walked in he came and sat at the front desk that was level with us, wearing neither his robes nor his wig. He did however, to me, look very 'judgelike' - old, grey and with sideburns to rival Elvis Presley. He sat down and put a file on his desk the thickness of three telephone books. He said hello and talked to the children for a few minutes, asking them if they had been on holiday. He also asked Julie if she knew why she was here, after a short silence she answered, "So that I can stay with mummy and daddy forever."

The judge then put on his robes and wig and we stood upon the higher platform to have our pictures taken. The judge then gave the children a bag each which contained sweets and toys, and us a certificate each showing the children's new names and adoption date.

After shaking the judge's hand, we left the courtroom and went back outside where we had our picture taken again, then we went into the shopping centre café for a coffee and chocolate muffin!

So now we are living as a complete family. Plans are underway for a christening, and the local pub is booked for a celebration afterwards. We decided that the children would have three godparents each, and chose Uncle Bill and Aunty Sophie, Uncle Jack and Aunty Sally and Aunty Terri. For the final Godparent we chose Uncle Dominic. Uncle Dominic is a very good friend of my husbands, and subsequently mine. He was the best man at our wedding ten years ago, and knew our situation with regard to not being able to have birth children of our own. After having a conversation with him about this one Sunday afternoon, Dominic turned to me and said, "I am sure it will happen in time Elaine, and you will have a family." At this I laughed and promised that when it happened, he would be called upon to be a godparent.

As with most friends, and even some family, we lost touch, over time and carried on with our lives. When we eventually decided that we would be christening our children, I got my husband to do a little digging to find a contact number for Dominic and that evening gave him a call. When he answered I said, "Hi Dom, It's Elaine, you know, Elaine and Ray?" He instantly remembered and asked how things were, to which I replied, "Things are great, you remember that promise I made to you nine years ago?" After what seemed like minutes of silence, things began to click into place and he said, "You haven't?" I began to tell him about the children we were adopting, whilst he was shrieking down the phone at me. A couple of weeks later he came to visit us and our children, who love him to bits. My only problem now was to decide who would be godparent to which child. I wrote it all down on paper, using all the different combinations that I could come up with, but nothing seemed right. On the 19th September I went to a meeting with the local Vicar to arrange the christening. Whilst there, I asked about the right and wrong ways to pick godparents. He already knew that the children were adopted as I had met him at the school governors meeting at the end of the summer term. I told him about the difficulty in choosing which people would be godparents to which child; I then hit upon an idea and ventured it forward. "Would there be any problem with all six people being godparents to both children?" The vicar thought for a moment and then smiled at me, "No," he said, "I cannot see a problem with that at all."

So, the church is booked, the pub is

booked, the invites have gone out and the cake has been ordered.

Julie moved up a class at the start of the new school year and continues to excel in her reading and writing. James began pre-school in September and enjoys every day. He is making friends and looking forward to joining Julie at her school in September 2006.

I decided to find a job that fitted in with my family. I was determined not to give up my role as a mother to someone charging an obscene amount of money so in May I became a Cosmetics Consultant and registered as self-employed. My job means that I can be there for my children at any time, and when I work, my husband is with the children. It gives me an extra income and the chance to meet new people as well as exercise my mind.

And what a day we had at the Christening! I had decided to do the buffet myself, and as it was on a Sunday, a local pub had said that we could have their 'best side' for our celebration afterwards. I spent the morning, and the night before, making sandwiches, buns, and finger food whilst wearing a pair of latex gloves, then ran around like an Olympic sprinter on the Sunday morning getting all the food to the pub. The landlady let me drop everything off at the pub's back doors and said that she would set everything out in time for when we arrived back from the church. I then took Julie in the car to pick up one of her school friends who we had said could come along.

At five to twelve, we all met in the church foyer, and then went in to sit down. Julie and James were the oldest children getting christened that day, but thoroughly enjoyed it all the same! We all stood around the font with the godparents and children while the vicar took each child to the font to baptise them, although he could not exactly pick up Julie and James and so he got them to stand on a stool. Afterwards, we all took it in turns to stand by the font with the children having our pictures taken. In one shot of the children on their own James decided to lean into the font and splash water on himself!

It had been raining all that Sunday morning but when we came out of the church, the sun appeared and began to shine. We arrived at the pub a few minutes later and the festivities began.

A friend of mine had got married a couple of years before and had bought a guest book for the occasion. Unfortunately, her wedding had been postponed and when she finally got married, the wedding was not as she had originally planned, and so the guest book went unused. She very kindly gave me the guest book, which I then took to the pub and got everyone who attended to sign the book. There have been some very moving messages written in the book, which I will treasure for a very long time.

After things had settled down, Anna arranged to visit the children and bring with her the Life Story Books that she had made for them. These books tell the children all about their life to date, about their three families, and explain in ways that they will understand, why they have been adopted. They are full of colourful pictures, but also contain the bad things as well as the good. These books are invaluable to us, and will always be available to the children.

Anna and I went thought Julie's book with her, while Ray took James out of the way, as at the moment he is too young to understand anything apart from the pictures. It is a lot easier for Julie as she has memories of her past families.

After going through the whole of the book, Anna went through it again at Julie's request, only this time Julie tried to skip all the 'bad' things and only concentrated on the good. This, as Anna later told me is 'classic behaviour'. In time, Julie will be able to go through the book accepting and understanding the bad things as much as the good. After all, the bad things are the reason why Julie's story is the way it is.

At this stage it was also important for me to stress to Anna that I did not want Julie to talk to James about their respective books, not yet. As James was only 22 months when he came to us, he has no memory or understanding of the 'other' families, and I feel that it should be mine and my husband's job to tell him when he is at a more appropriate age, rather than Julie telling him all about it and confusing him as this early stage.

That is a job that part of me is not looking forward to. However, when the time arrives I know we will always have the support of the after adoption team from the Adoption Agency, and - if need be - I am sure Anna will be able to offer advice as she knows the children so well, although by then, her work with us will have been completed.

We have also been given Later Life Letters, from Anna, one for each of our children. These letters explain things in a little more detail, but are for when the children are a little older. They do not contain any pictures, but instead are a more detailed description of our children's birth family, a sort of who's who, who did what and why. I have put these letters with the children's life story books; although I know that I will not be giving them to the children until they have a much better understanding of the whole concept of adoption and what it entails. At the moment, I think that these letters will be shared with my children when they reach the ages of 11 or 12, but maybe in the future things will change that will cause me to get them out earlier or later. Whatever happens, Ray and I have promised that these letters will be shared with our children before they reach the age of 18.

Preparations have also been made to contact certain members of our children's birth family through the letterbox scheme. This scheme means that I can write to these family members via the adoption agency. After checking that the letters contain no references to who we are or where we live, the letters are then passed to the birth family members who then reply via the same agency, which means that they and us have no way of tracing each-other, but we each keep updated.

Again, I will keep any letters that I receive with a view to sharing these with the children when they are at an age of understanding and if they want to see them. After all, they may decide that they do not want to see them.

Christmas this year was fantastic. We had decided that we would spend it on our own, and would break the usual Boxing Day tradition by not going to a hotel for lunch. We stored all the wrapped presents at Uncle Bill and Aunty Sophie's house across the road. After the children had drifted to sleep on Christmas Eve we fetched all the gifts back home and set them out in the living room, this time making sure that they were in individual piles, one for Julie, one for James and one for me and my husband. The next morning we got up, got the children dressed and were about to come downstairs when I realised that I had not put Santa's glitter footsteps on the hall floor as I had the previous year, so I told the children to wait at the top of the stairs in the dark with Dad while I went down to take a look, and get the camcorder ready. As I loaded the camcorder I called upstairs to say that Santa had not been. I quickly got the pot of glitter and began sprinkling it on the floor. Still calling up the stairs that there were no presents, I went into the living room and jangled the bell on Julie's Christmas stocking, the children heard the bell and, according to my husband their faces lit up. Then I called in a deep voice, "Ho, Ho, Ho, sorry I am a bit late," back in my own voice, I told 'Santa' "No problem, thanks for coming," then back in Santa's voice I boomed, "Merry Christmas!" and pretended to shut the back door behind him, then I called to the children, "Quick, come down, Santa's just left!" The children raced downstairs as I switched the camera to record, and they began to open their presents.

Uncle Bill and Aunty Sophie came across mid-morning with the excuse that Santa had left some presents for the children at their house and once again Julie and James began ripping paper left right and centre. After dinner, we spent the afternoon playing with the children and their new toys; Boxing Day was much the same apart from taking a break to go for a walk. Afterwards my husband commented that it was one of the best Christmases that he had ever had. The children were more than content with what they had received and played happily whilst we watched.

And so another new year arrived, no doubt a year that will be filled with highs and lows. James will be starting infant school this September and is looking forward to making lots of new friends. Julie will continue to improve dramatically with reading and writing, and as a family things can only get better.

There will always be bad days, and there will always be good days, and just lately we are starting to see brilliant days.

But at the moment I have a wonderful husband, two adorable children and all the support I need. Life does not get any better than this.

The End
(of the beginning).

Epilogue

2005 TO 2012

As time passed, my parents became more distant. We had never been in each other's pockets, but their ideas concerning raising children were very different to mine. I had to take a myriad of things into account whilst raising my adopted children, things that my mother and step father were unable to fully understand and arguments followed.

One such disagreement concerned food. At 2 years old, James was eating regular meals; in fact, he had not eaten baby food since before he was placed with us, yet every time we were at my parents' house, they insisted on liquidizing his meal and feeding him slop. No matter how many times I tried to talk about this, I was met with a glare from my mother that seemed to say "You are not a mother, how would you know how to raise children?"

I tried to hold onto the love I had for my parents, particularly my mother, but the more she dug her heels in, the more I dug mine in too. These children had been given to Ray and me after two years of formal parental training. Surely I knew what I was doing. After all, she had only had one child, was divorced and re-married before I turned three years old.

In my eyes, she took every opportunity to separate me from my children. She never did as I asked as far as they were concerned and on the few occasions I let the children stay overnight at her house, I had to take James' travel cot, sheets, blankets, clothes, dishes, baby cutlery, nappies, wipes plus a camp bed and bedding for Julie, as my mother flatly refused to keep anything in her home, and refused to let Julie sleep in their spare bed.

On one occasion, I think it was the first time they took Julie and James away for a few days, I gave my mother a list of do's and don'ts. She didn't even read it, just scanned it quickly, screwed it up and threw it in the rubbish bin while I sat there and watched. She even went as far as to say to my children in front of me, "Your mother's stupid." Whether she was joking or not I don't know, but you don't say things like that to six and two year olds.

Having a relationship with my mother was becoming more of a chore, and I began to resent her remarks and questioning of my parenting abilities.

My maternal Grandfather had been ill for a long time and by now was in a nursing home. Unbeknownst to me, my mother and step father had gone away on holiday and had left my contact details at the nursing home. The home rang me just as Anna (Julie and James' social worker) was finishing one of her visits and I raced off to see what was happening. I can't remember exactly what was wrong with Granddad, I had never been told the full extent of his illness, but I think cancer was involved. He was lying in bed, no teeth, a shell of a man, eyes closed, and dying. The nurses at the home had phoned for his doctor to come out, but he had refused saying that there was nothing that he could do. The home called a locum who attended while I was there. He came, then, took me into another room to explain what was happening. His words washed over me, nothing sunk in, except that this was my Granddads' time, and he probably wouldn't make it through the night. Staff at the nursing home contacted his brothers who came with their wives and sat with me until late. We reminisced about when I and they were younger, with Granddads rattling breath the only other sound in the room. Every so often Granddad would raise his hand towards the corner of the ceiling. I, and the four people with me, came to the conclusion that someone from heaven had come to collect him, and that he was telling them "I'm on my way." It was the only thought that kept us going.

I telephoned my mother, whose cold words of "I am at the caravan, I am not coming home early, the funeral directors have been paid already they know what do," left a horrible shiver down my spine, how could she be so cold? I know she never got on with her father but even so, he was her father.

We left at 11pm with instructions to the nurses to contact me if anything happened. Granddads' brothers and sisters-in-law had asked that I contact them too.

I was woken at half past three the next morning to go down to the nursing home as Granddad was fading fast. I arrived at four the Matron was waiting for me. She rushed me up the stairs but it was too late, I had missed him by minutes. I was numb.

As his own doctor had refused to visit him, I had to wait for the police to arrive so that I could identify his body, then his brothers and sisters-in-law arrived, and shortly afterwards, I went home.

The nursing home contacted the funeral directors and they took over. My mother did come home early, but only for one day and only to finalise arrangements. She then returned to her holiday telling the funeral directors that the service could wait until she returned from her holiday a week later.

This was the straw that broke the donkey's

back for Ray. "That's it, if you want a relationship with your parents that's up to you, I won't stop you, but don't you ever take my children anywhere near them."

I agreed with him.

I went to the service on my own driving to my parents' house so that I could travel in the funeral car. I didn't speak to my parents except to say "Oh," when shown a photo of a new-born family member. Granddad was cremated, there was no wake afterwards. My mother asked my Nan about going back with them for a cup of tea, I don't think my Grandmother really understood what was going on at the time. But my mother never asked me, it was actually Lucy who invited me, and I just politely declined.

The funeral car pulled up at my parents' house, and I was back in my own car and on my way home before they had even reached the front door. That's when I decided that I needed to cut ties with my family. They would never be the kind of parents I wanted them to be and I could never be the kind of daughter they expected me to be. I cried all the way home, it was the hardest decision of my life but I had no choice.

We moved in 2007, a hundred and twenty three miles away to the coast. We found a lovely school for our children and they settled in well. I got a small job in a school and began running a crafts club at my children's primary school. I have a small circle of close friends who accepted me and my family into their community.

Lucy is now married and has a step daughter of her own. We have trips down see her, or they come and stay with us.

The children continue to grow and flourish. Yes we had problems. Julie has short term memory loss, with which the school has been helping us. And James began to show challenging behaviour. But essentially, they are both bright and happy. Julie is the more arty of the two. She will happily draw or paint, and enjoys crafts, and now at nearly 14, she is discovering boys, make-up and pushing boundaries.

James, at 10, is more academic. He's not fussed about drawing, but is very bright when it comes to maths. He's a great problem solver, but will scheme and go to great lengths to get what he wants. He's always getting himself into some kind of mischief and can run rings around me when it comes to playing tennis on the Wii.

We are a family. We are doing what families do, taking each day one at a time, and whatever comes our way, we will face it together.

As a family.

Printed in Great Britain
by Amazon